I0833571

Raven Blair Davis

Praise For

Broadcast Your Passion To Profits

“Most people are sitting on a goldmine and don't even know it. By applying the simple strategies in “Broadcast Your Passion To Profits,” you can quickly create multiple streams of income, boost your celebrity status, and increase your time off using the untapped resources already at your disposal. No matter if you are an entrepreneur, student, work-at-home parent, or retiree; you will discover the perfect way to turn your passion into wealth."

William R. Patterson
Award-Winning Speaker, Business and Wealth Coach
National Bestselling Co-author of *The Baron Son*

“In her exciting new book, “Broadcast Your Passion To Profits,” Raven Blair Davis shares her vast knowledge and advice on the in’s and out’s of starting your own internet radio talk show. “Broadcast Your Passion To Profits” is a very specific, simple and concise informational book covering all aspects of starting to make the dream of your own talk show come true. But most importantly Raven sprinkles vital bits of inspiration and wisdom throughout in this perfect guide to the internet radio talk show market”

Debbie Zipp
In the Trenches Productions.com

“Raven Blair Davis book "Broadcast Your Passion To Profits" is a must read. They say timing is everything, so is this book! With the economy falling apart and people looking for tools for new ideas, this book will inspire and motivate you to do what your heart desires. This wonderful book should be in every home. Tune in to the written content and I bet you the value you receive will be far more than your investment!”

Gregory Norman
CEO Universal 7 Radio Network, 1320 WARL AM

“This is an excellent book about the world of broadcasting on the internet. It provides a step to step guide which is introspective and offers inspiring quotes between each chapter which are food for thought. Take a look through the eyes of an experienced podcaster and learn from the best."

S Cuppari

***Writing Edge* - The lifestyle magazine for writers**

Broadcast your Passion to Profits
Published by Raven Blair Davis

Library of Congress Cataloging-in-Publication Data:

Cover Design by Carolyn Sheltraw

Blair Davis, Raven
Broadcast your Passion to Profits
/ Raven Blair Davis
ISBN 978-1-4495205-6-4

1. Broadcasting 2. Purpose

Printed in the United States of America

TABLE OF CONTENTS

"I can do all

Things through Christ

Who Strengthens Me"

Philippines 4:13

Dedication

This book is dedicated to my loving husband, Larry, for his undeniable support and for the belief he's always had in me even during the times I could not see the full picture for being in the frame. Thank you for always being there and believing Larry - I love you dearly!

Also I want to dedicate this book to some very dear family members that are no longer here but I choose to believe they are in heaven smiling at this moment and I've felt their presence along the way. To my adorable, sweet father, Lloyd Blair, whom I love so very much and who taught me the true meaning of always giving your best. To my loving in laws Lillian Davis who had so much personality and humor, and my father in law Rayford Davis who was a dynamic speaker and put the speak in "speaker."

Lastly, I dedicate this book to my niece in law, if there is such a thing, Nikki Drake whose charm and smile will always be remembered. And to Aunt Dez who always displayed so much courage and strength and was always positive despite the odds – she never gave up.

I love and miss you all so much and I am grateful for the love you gave me and for the memories you left behind.

Raven Blair Davis

ACKNOWLEDGEMENTS

I am so thankful for my family. We're very small but close and supportive of each other. I feel blessed to have all of you in my life.

Thank you Mom, you always knew even when I was not sure that I could be more if I tried harder, you taught me how to be spectacular selling and communicating over the telephone and now it's paid off big time. Thank you for that and for all your love and support. When you were in the hospital and going through pain, I was forced to sit still and at the same time I woke up and realized the true value of life. It's because of you MOM, that I had the strength and the inspiration to change my life's destiny. I love you so much Mom!

To my brother Lloyd Jr. and my sister Renee in Cleveland who I miss and love very much. Special thanks to my son in law John and precious daughter, Jaemi, for always giving me that extra encouragement I need when I need it the most. A very special thanks to my grandson, Christian, for believing in me and to my son, Adam (Blair), you are such a caring young man, and you're always there when the family needs you. Thank you for always being there I appreciate you so very much!

Also I want to thank Parish, my precious niece; you have been so much help and encouragement. I am grateful to have you as my program director. Thank you to my nephew, Rasheen (aka Extraordinaire), for your words of encouragement, I can't wait to read your first book.

I especially want to thank from the bottom of my heart, my sister, Tracey Doctor. You have been through so much and have given much more than you've received. Because you have been there with Mom for the past three years at the hospital and at home, it's allowed me to pursue the vision of having a radio network that would empower and inspire boomer women and men to live their dreams and unleash their greatness. I cannot put into words,

Tracey, what you mean to me and to the whole family and how grateful we all are for all that you have given and for the love, support and kindness you have shown Mom during her illness. Thank you Sis you are truly an Amazing Woman.

I would like to thank all those who assisted me along my journey. There were and are so many people that have made my vision as a talk show host come alive and grow larger than I could imagine. First I could not begin my thank you without acknowledging those closest to me that have seen me and comforted me through the down time and the struggles and gave me all they could in knowledge, time, product and services. I was never missing anything I truly needed. WOW, as I think back I have truly been blessed and I am grateful for my family and for you.

To my longtime and dear friends Cinnamon, Tina, Charles Etta, George, Rita, Ronnie, Mary and James (Junior) I thank and acknowledge you for being a very special part of my life. For the many years you have been and remain my friends even when I was too busy to visit or to just stop for a moment and pick up the phone to say hello. I appreciate your friendship, patience and understanding. Thank you for your true friendship and for being there the many times I needed you. I love you all.

Very special thanks go to Qarlah Prince. You were my very first advertiser for Women Power and mentor; you're truly an extraordinary and gifted negotiator, business woman, author, speaker and talk show host but most of all you are an extraordinary friend...the best. Thank you for all that you have passed on to me.

My dear friend, producer and business partner, Regina Baker, I appreciate all the technical work you've done to give me a larger and impressive presence on the internet.
You friendship, support, and wisdom has been invaluable I appreciate you so very much.

Greg Norman, you have taking me under your wing and because of that I've learned so much along the way and have learned to expect miracles and to "act as if" for that I say...thank you my friend.

My dear friend Kimberly Rhodes, I've learned so much from you in branding, creating products and marketing. Thanks for your friendship and your many words of wisdom.

Lisa Kitter, once I began to be personally coached by you I couldn't help but get enthusiastic about getting my message out, about assisting others to get past their adversities about making a difference. I love your enthusiasm. Also thanks for introducing me to my first virtual assistant, Suzanne, who I also want to thank for giving me a dynamic website presence when I had not much to give you except a promise to do what I could. I'll never forget you and I am so glad you believed in me. Tracy McCarthy you have assisted me with many technical issues and you are always there ready to step in and help when I need you even on short notice I so appreciate you for all that you do. Karen Salter of Salter Virtual Assistants, I understand why you always win those numerous awards ... you are indeed good at what you do. I appreciate the work you have done in assisting me with all of my products - you're AWESOME!!!

Thank you, Donald Wells. You're always so positive and so encouraging. You know how to give me that tough love when I need it and I appreciate you my friend.
My dear friend Marcia Merrill, you flew to Houston twice to help me prepare for my Kitchen Table Radio course. I will never forget what you did my friend I miss you much.

Finally I want to thank Alex Mandossian, Les Brown, Cynthia Kersey, Wendy Salahuddin, Jack Canfield, Lisa Kitter and Karen Copeland for your mentoring, your teachings, your message, your audios, and your books. All of you have been extremely instrumental in me making a complete U-turn in my life. You will always be not only my mentors but my heroes. Thank you for all that you've done in assisting me and the millions you have assisted or will assist around the world.

Last but definitely not least, thank you to all my loyal listeners and guests that have supported all of my shows especially my first guest, Brenda Graff, and my first celebrity, Jayne Kennedy Overton. I appreciate your contribution to the show and the encouragement you gave me early on in my journey.
Thank you!

WOW, I've learned along my journey that life is full of surprise and opportunities. You never know who you'll meet via the telephone, internet or in person that will take you to the next step in fulfilling your dream. To anyone who is reading this, I say believe in your dream and the people who will enter your life, to help you develop along the way, and to help take you where you want to go. Remember them, appreciate them, and be in gratitude but most importantly be sure you pay it forward so in the future you will be on someone else's gratitude list and they, my friend, will be thanking you in their first book. How cool is that!

FOREWORD

Thank you, Raven Blair Davis for creating yet another medium to help "just normal" people realize there is no such thing as "just normal!" *Broadcast Your Passion To Profits* is a beautifully written inspirational guide with loads of good information. But, it is also a short and snappy memoir that gives readers the wonderful opportunity to know a little more about what drives this amazing podcast diva.

Readers not only learn how Raven Blair Davis miraculously changed her own life; but, how anyone with a passion to change, can do just that. *Broadcast Your Passion To Profits* is a shot in the arm for any woman or man who fails to see their possibilities, only their failures. *Broadcast Your Passion To Profits* impels readers to get rid of their sense of being passive victims, and instead: Claim their legacies, now! "

Thank you Raven Blair Davis, for *Broadcast Your Passion To Profits*! It is the push that both women and men need, to begin our lives again, and to leave a legacy in this fast-paced cyber world.

Janis F. Kearney
Former Presidential Diarist, for Bill Clinton
Author, Publisher, International Speaker, *Writing our World Press*

"Unleash the power of your voice and let your message be heard!

Yes, it's YOUR TIME TO SHINE"

Raven Blair Davis

Utilizing the Audio/Podcast Innovations in Your Business

There is power in your voice, I kid you not. Eighty percent of people remember what they hear; twenty percent remember what they read. Sarah Palin, CNN, Business Week, 60 Minutes, the BBC, Best of Today, ESPN, Barack Obama, and John McCain all have or previously had a podcast. Podcast is the new era. It's what's going on, it's here, it's now, and it is not going away.

In fact, it's rapidly growing momentum all around the world. In 2007, the market estimated that the total US podcast audience reached 16.5 million. In 2008, Arbitron media research released that 29 million people are listening to podcasts all over the world. The great news is the United States spending on podcast related advertising, including sponsorship, is expected to rise to four hundred thirty five million dollars by 2012. This is what every business should be doing. Every single business; big, small, just getting started, or thinking about getting started, should all be podcasting.

I am so excited that you have decided to investigate podcasting as a tool to grow your business! Just when you thought you had a handle on all the opportunities the internet provided, you suddenly find yourself faced with a new one – an audio revolution. Yes, the internet evolved from one that gave us quick and easy written content and is now moving us into another dimension with audio content.

Then internet radio was born, which paved the path for the podcasting development. The audio progression on the internet proved to be more of an opportunity for business owners than was ever originally thought. It was not only a hobby or casual past time but proved to be a dynamic way to get YOUR message out. It enabled you to communicate your passion to the world, whether it is something as serious as cancer treatment, abuse prevention or something else you are passionate about like golf, finance, real estate, business and marketing strategies, etc. I could go on and on the list is endless.

Before I continue with why I feel every business owner should be broadcasting their passion/message to profits, let me introduce myself. My name is Raven Blair Davis and I am the creator of three Internet radio talk shows:

Women Power Talk Radio
Mentoring from MLM Divas Live
Careers from the Kitchen Table

Women Power Radio is targeted at women over forty, Mentoring from MLM Divas Live is targeted at women in network marketing and Careers from The Kitchen Table is for the home business enthusiast as well as those looking to take their career from corporate to working at home.

In addition, I have well over twenty-five years in telephone sales, customer service, marketing and management. I have been responsible for training and coaching hundreds of people in the industry and have won many awards throughout my career with such Fortune 500 hundred companies as MCI and Cendant.

I was born and raised in Cleveland, Ohio and now live in Houston, Texas with my wonderful and supportive husband, Larry. My mission is to assist women over forty in designing and pursuing their passions and dreams despite their age, setbacks, challenges or any perceived limitations. I feel you can do any job and create any business once you learn to master the art of tele-connecting.

A lot of people miss the fact that their business can grow exponentially by using a simple tool that we all have in our homes and even in our cars – the Telephone! You can use the internet to build relationships but many people are missing the fact that you can truly build lasting relationships by picking up the phone and talking to people. Find out what you can do FOR them – not what they can do for you. Once I mastered the art of tele-connecting, it really assisted me in booking experts, celebrities and gurus to be on my shows as well as getting testimonials from them. This can really elevate your business quickly. Tele-connecting has also assisted me in making new friends that have become very dear to me like Diana Nightingale (widow of the great Earl Nightingale), Claudette Robinson (the First Lady of Motown and formerly married to Smokey Robinson), as well as Iris Gordy, the niece of the legendary founder of Motown's Berry Gordy, Wally Amos, founder of The Famous Amos cookies and many, many others.

WHERE AND HOW IT ALL BEGAN

My journey into radio began at a very bleak moment in my life. My Mom was extremely ill and was in the hospital for six months. Fear lurked in the corridors of the ICU Ward within the walls of Methodist Hospital while the woman who nurtured and protected me lay still and quiet. I spent weeks in darkness, watching her with all the tubes and equipment around her and I began to wonder. *"Is she going to make it? Is my Mom going to live or is God ready to take her home?"*

There is so much quiet time when you are faced with endless hours waiting in a hospital! As your mind will do in desperate times, I started reviewing her life and I found myself asking questions.
Had Mom done the things she wanted to do in her life? Had she reached her goals? Had she reached her dreams? Had Mom done the things that she wanted –traveled to places she always dreamed of, had she obtained her goals? Was she living the life that she wanted to live or was she living her life trying to please my Dad, myself and my siblings?

As the days and nights grew into weeks and then months, I started asking myself the same questions. To my despair, the answer was no to every question. I wasn't living my dream. I hadn't really done anything. Not anything that I felt was important or exciting. I felt I wasn't leaving any kind of legacy. Where was the little girl that *KNEW* she was going to be somebody? What had happened to the adventurous young Raven who stood for hours in the shadows of the radio station amazed with the turntables and thrilled at the DJ's banter? Was she a failure?

That really started to bother me. During my quiet times, I kept thinking and returning to the same questions. I kept digging for the Raven with hopes, dreams and high ambitions. Where was she? Why had I settled for less in life and given up on my dreams? It was during one of those times that God placed it on my heart that it was time for me to make a difference. It was time for me to stop taking from this good earth and start giving back.

So my next question was, *"How am I going to do it?"* I was just an ordinary woman who had never done anything that extraordinary. I hadn't written a book or even a magazine article! My background was in telesales, telemarketing and management. Then I remembered something from Alex Mandossian's Teleseminar Secrets course. He mentioned interviewing experts. I thought, *"I can talk. I'm good at that!"* Finally, I can put those years of telemarketing to good use!

I decided I wanted to empower women like me. They are the boomer women - in their 40's, 50's, 60's and up. They haven't quite reached their dreams and their visions. These women have had setbacks like me, challenges like me, and, just like me, they found themselves settling in life and giving up on their dreams. I started to really focus, zoom in and meditate on that. I listened to my inner voice and let it guide me. Finally I said, *"That's it!"* Boomer women and the men who love them need a voice, they need encouragement, and they need inspiration. I am going to go out there and interview dynamic experts who are also boomers.

I wanted to get extraordinary women to come on my show and share not only their successes but their how to's. My audience needs to know that they don't have to settle for where they are in life. My goal was to help them see they can create their dreams. They can get through their trials and tribulations and turn them into triumphs.

So I created *Women Power Talk Radio* right at the Methodist hospital! It was created there, formatted there and I even recorded a couple shows there! I began to realize what Napoleon Hill said was indeed true. If you can conceive it and believe it you can certainly achieve it! I was now beginning to be living proof of it.

Then it went from one show to another. My husband, Larry and I were in network marketing. We were able to plug into incredible mentors at seminars and realized it was really valuable. However, even though statistics showed the majority of network marketers were women, the majority of the leaders and highly successful presenters were men. The women who came across the stage, while few, were extremely successful and powerful. I thought it would be great if more women were on that stage as mentors for all women in the MLM arena. There were many women at the seminar but not very many leaders. So *Mentoring From MLM Divas Live* was born to get the women who had been there, done that and were very successful in the industry, to come on and share their real secrets, tips and know how without promoting their company or their product. To give back to the industry and help more women accomplish what they had accomplished. To help more women become prominent in the industry and be leaders. To not just be behind the scenes but become successful and be a leader.

My third show was conceived in the spring of 2007. I received an email from Greg Norman, founder of Universal 7 Network on 1320 WARL A.M. saying how much he enjoyed listening to my Women Power celebrity interview with Jayne Kennedy (yes I got to interview one of my childhood idols!). He wanted to talk to me about bringing the show over to his station. At first when I spoke to him that was the plan. But then the wheels started turning again.

I started thinking about how many people were losing their jobs, being laid off, down sized or forced into early retirement. Many boomer women and boomer men were starting to feel out of place at their jobs or they were mistreated in such a way it was becoming impossible to continue working.

After really thinking about that and remembering how I once felt, I decided that it would be more of a benefit to WARL listeners if they knew they had options. They could easily start a business from home while they were working so that if something ever happened and they found themselves suddenly out of work they would have a plan "B" already in place. I wanted to give them a weekly show they could plug into that would lay out a step by step plan. I would present them with experts, and gurus from all over the world like Jack Canfield, Les Brown, Diana Nightingale, Dr. Joe Vitale, Lisa Nichols, Regina Baker, Mark Victor Hansen, Ali Brown, Michael Senoff, Terri Levine and so many others. They would mentor them to creating, launching, marketing effectively as well as growing and maintaining a successful and profitable home base business. This would be known as the show to listen to that would give world-wide listeners ideas of different business opportunities available they could partner themselves with, as well as some work at home jobs. My goal was to give them ideas on how they could take any passion, hobby or expertise they had and turn it into a business that they could work from home and would take them from the hectic highway to the smooth sailing hallway working in their PJ's if they want, right from their kitchen table.

Careers from the Kitchen Table was born! At the time, I didn't realize it would be the perfect solution for the economic challenges we were about to face. We created the show because we thought it was important for people to know how to create income for themselves and begin a plan B while still at their job. Now we find ourselves in the middle of a recession. Jobs are more important than ever and taking the risk to start a home business may not be the perfect solution at this time. But, the idea of the show is to encourage listeners to build their home business while they still have a job so they will have something to fall back on if they lose that job.

Listeners learn how simple it can be to create or generate income from home without maxing out their credit cards or selling their home to get started. And they get to hear specific strategies and formulas for success from the best of the best that they could begin to put into action ....immediately if they wanted success bad enough. I knew in my heart this type of show was needed and would be appreciated and so it was!

"We can only do what we think we can do.
We can be only what we think we can be.
We can have only what we think we can have.
What we do, what we are, what we have, all depends upon what we think."

Robert Collier

"What is Internet Radio and Podcasting?"

Internet radio was developed in the early 1990's for informational as well as entertainment purposes. It was a simple means of bringing the radio to the internet, but some users found it cumbersome with having to retrieve the content through one file at a time.

Over the years, internet radio developed to become a media outlet brought by internet streaming media programs such as MP3's etc. Users found this to be much more reliable and flexible as they could download the shows and listen to them later on.

Podcasting came along when RSS feeds were widely popular. It was found that one could provide audio content to users by delivering it via these feeds. This enabled a user to download the content onto their portable media players as well as their computers. One could listen to the podcast whenever and wherever they wanted without being constricted to their computer. The convenience this provided was one of the reasons this media option became so popular.

"On demand radio," means listeners can tune in at their convenience, download your show and take you right along with them while they shop, jog or at little Johnny's soccer game. How sweet it is!

Podcasting is generally pre-recorded in smaller segments and then uploaded for any user to access when they choose to. This allows for more options in content and programming than radio since editing can make your segments be exactly what you want them to be.

THE HISTORY OF PODCASTING

The term "Podcasting" has only been around since 2004. The Internet has allowed many movements to occur in the last decade, and there is no doubt that podcasting would have emerged sooner or later, but it was spurred on by a small collection of individuals.

One of them was Adam Curry. In 2004, Curry was working as a DJ at Radio Veronica in the Netherlands. When he was not on the air he was working on developing a computer application by tinkering with some computer code in a language called AppleScript. The script collected audio files from different sources on the Internet, and he automatically loaded them onto his iPod so he could listen to them at his leisure. He dubbed the code iPodder, and released the first version to the public on August 15, 2004.

Curry had the idea for the computer program for several years, and had mentioned its application to some programmers in the hope they'd develop it. Very few had been interested, and so, out of frustration, he began learning what he needed to write the code himself.

Enter Curry's friend, Dave Winer, whom he'd first met in the mid-nineties. Winer helped to create several different companies and many different technologies that defined computing. He started the company *Living*

Videotext, which was sold to *Symantec* for a tidy penny, and later started another company called *Userland Software*. This established him as a driving force in the popularity of weblogs, because of its blog software called *Radio Userland* (which was originally created as a music sharing system).

Winer was one of several people that helped develop Really Simple Syndication (RSS). Its purpose was to make it easy for anyone to receive information over a computer network like the Internet: basically a really simple way to syndicate information. It's now widely adopted by online news providers, like newspapers, magazine, and weblogs, so anyone can easily subscribe to their updates, known as a feed.

After meeting with Curry in January of 2001, Winer added one simple element to his RSS specification called an enclosure. This was a way to include a multimedia payload into a feed. Publishers could now include video or audio in their syndications.

RSS first became popular with authors of the written word. Online newspapers, magazines, and weblogs used the code to improve the usability of their websites. This led to the development of readers that allowed internet users to subscribe to an RSS feed, which would deliver the information straight to their computer on a regular basis.

Quick Facts

- **November 2001** – The first iPod sold.

- **September 2004** - Google had less than 25 hits for the search term "Podcasting".

- **September 2005** - Google hits for search term "Podcasting" = 61 million!

- **2005** - Scheduled or branded podcasts jumped from just a few shows to more than 3,500 combined with more than 2,500 Internet audio streams of regular radio station broadcasts!

- **2007** - EMarketer estimates that the total US podcast audience reached 18.5 million. Driven by this audience growth, US spending on podcast-related advertising (including sponsorships) will rise to $435 million in 2012, up from $165 million in 2007.

- **April 9, 2007** - Apple® announced that the 100 millionth iPod® has been sold.

- **January 2008** - Arbitron-Edison Media Research study found that an estimated 33 million Americans had listened to online radio in the past week. This represents 13% of the US population ages 12 and older, and is an increase over the previous year when 11% of the population (29 million) had listened to online radio in the past week.

- **2008 and 2009** – *Women Power Radio* name one of the Top 100 Podcast by Small *Business Trends Radio*. http://www.smbtrendwire.com

Podcast.com Top 10 Podcasts 2007

- World Soccer Daily
- CNN News Update
- ESPN Radio Daily
- Geek News Central Podcast
- BBC's Best of Today
- Nova – PBS
- Slate Magazine Daily Podcast
- 60 Minutes Podcast - The Full Broadcast
- Face the Nation Podcast
- CNET News.com

"Champions aren't made in gyms champions are made from something that they have deep, deep inside of them, a burning desire, a lofty dream and an unstoppable vision. They have to have the skill and they have to have the will. But the will must be far stronger than the skill."

Muhammad Ali

Benefits For Both Online and Offline Businesses

Podcasting was always known as a great medium for informational purposes and entertainment as well as mentioned earlier to share your passion with the world but it has also become an even greater tool to use for marketing any online and offline business. Political candidates, such as McCain and Obama, had podcasts during the campaign because they realize Americans are continually on the move and may not take the time to watch TV but they will download information to their iPod to listen to at their convenience.

You can podcast audio and/or video, the choice is yours. It can be from a one minute tip to an hour long interview. The most popular length is 20 minutes because that is the length of the average commute which is a popular time for listeners to tune in.

Here are some benefits your business could be rewarded with through the use of podcasting:

- **Popularity in your field**. If your podcast becomes a successful one, internet users will keep coming back for more and more.

- **Your business credibility and trust builds** quickly with potential customers and your name inevitably becomes synonymous with your particular business field.

- **Increased traffic**- The more users that tune into your podcasts, the more traffic you could receive that would want to check out your business site and see what you have to offer them.

- **Edging out Competition**. While podcasting is popular today; most business owners still don't use this medium to market themselves. By taking on the podcasting revolution, you can rise above your competitors easily. Clients or customers will remember you far more often, when they need a product or service in your field, than any of your competitors.

- **Promote and advertise your business globally**. The quickest way to advertise your products is through a podcast. Simply record a podcast offering information about the product and those who have subscribed to your feed can have instant access to it. You can easily have someone create a commercial about any of your products or services in your podcast and you can edit it into your podcast sending listeners back to your website to purchase your book, coaching, workshops, even hire you to come speak for their organization from all over the world. Now that's exciting!

- **Attract Customers and Clients**. Almost by default! People will find your podcast on iTunes or the Web and will become interested in your product or service without you ever mentioning it. Then they will subscribe to your list and buy your product or service because they will see you as an expert in your field.

- **Retain Your Current Customers** - You will also retain current clients because they will know they have a place to visit to find updates on your new products or services and tips on how to use your services. They will be lifelong customers because they can go to your podcast and find information they need. So now your customers cannot only visit your website or place of business but they can download your podcast and take you with them – on their daily commute, their jog and even their job. It is more personal and you become a friend and not only a vendor.

- **Generate Additional Streams of Income** – Obtain advertisers or sponsors for your podcast. You may have current clients who would pay you to place their advertisement on your podcast. They are trying to reach the same target market as you. Your current suppliers may also wish to purchase advertising.

- **Search Engine Friendly.** Podcasting provides those search engine web crawlers with link popularity and fresh content on a regular basis.

With all the marketing tools available to choose from, podcasting should be one of them. It's one of the best ways to give internet users a different medium while making their experience a more interactive one.

"You can be whatever you want to be. There is inside you all of the potential to be whatever you want to be. All of the Energy to do whatever you want to do. Imagine yourself as you would like to be doing what you want to do and then each day take one step toward your dream. And though at times it may seem TOO difficult to continue, hold on to your dream. One morning you are going to awake to find that you are the person you dreamed of and that you are truly doing what you wanted to do. Yes, for you your vision has come true simply because you had the courage to believe in your potential and the strength, despite your challenge, to hold on to your dream."

Donna Levine

Finding Your Passion

Launching your own show doesn't have to be a frightening experience for you. Keep in mind; we're not talking about recording a live radio show broadcasted on the am/fm air waves of your car or home radios. This is a downloadable Internet medium that already has the foundation for what you need.

The biggest challenge when starting your own podcast is thinking you have to get it perfect. Just get out there and do it! Don't wait until you have all the answers because you're never going to have all the answers. I think a lot of people don't reach their true destiny in their business because they are so worried about trying to get it perfect along the way. They're scared to get to the next step because they don't have the current step perfect.

Discover your true passion or purpose. Ask yourself the following questions.

- What makes you so happy and excited that you want to jump out of bed in the morning?
- What lit you up as a child?
- What message or cause do you have a burning desire to share?

- What have you always wanted to do?

- What is your real reason for doing this?

Knowing the answer to these questions is the beginning process for creating your podcast. You need to know your WHY.

When I started creating my show, I knew I wanted to reach women like myself, women over forty, the baby boomers, and even older women. I knew it was important for me to assist women who felt like I did. These are women who felt they hadn't really reached their goals and their dreams. They felt like they were settling and they wanted more out of life.

My parents always wanted the best for me but my upbringing was very strict. Having goals or dreams wasn't always encouraged. Little did I know that the strict way I was raised would become the culprit for my life obstacles! This would trigger a lot of self-doubt, low self esteem, and little hope in accomplishing my dreams. As I became an adult, I grew accustomed to settling for what I had in life. I began to believe that whatever I had was exactly what I deserved...and nothing more.

But somehow I often found myself wondering, why not me? Why can't I have more? I began to read books like *Think and Grow Rich*, by Napoleon Hill, *The Game of Life and How to Play It* by Florence Skoval Shin, and *Unstoppable* by Cynthia Kersey. I really enjoyed the inspirational stories

Cynthia told of people who at one time had very little in life. Who, because of their strong will and determination, were now best-selling authors, extraordinary athletes, and highly successful business owners. I began to buy more books and soon had a library. I added CDs and DVDs containing incredible stories that inspired me. I attended seminars to learn from famous luminaries from all over the world, and I began to have hope again. I started dreaming again. It felt absolutely wonderful! But after about four years, I noticed I had not seen much progress or change. I was still living day-to-day. Other than learning from some dynamic people, I had not seen much of a difference in my life. Frustration and disappointment set in.

I had never written a book. My background was in telesales, telemarketing and management. I was frustrated and scared because I thought *"How am I going to do anything this huge when I am not well known in the business industry, I wasn't a speaker and I hadn't written a book, who would be interested in what I have to say?"* That's when I enrolled in Alex Mandossian's Tele-seminar Secret Course. One day when I called from the hospital to listen in on his live class, I heard Alex mentioned that the quickest way to go from unknown to expert status is by interviewing experts. I thought, 'I can talk! I can do that!' I found my passion.

Raymond Holliwell once said, "Desire creates the power." I truly believe that. You must know and understand your purpose and know exactly what your message is. It's important that you have a real clear vision of the type of show you want to produce and the market you want to reach.

Next are some tips that assisted me in getting started quickly and effectively, on a shoe string budget right from my kitchen table. How cool is that!

SEVEN FAST ACTION STEPS FOR STARTING YOUR OWN PODCAST

1. **Identify your Target Market and Message.** Start with your message. What is your message? How far do I want to take this message? Locally, state to state, or global? It's important to take your time to do that. Then identify who your market is. You may already have your own business, so you know what your message is and who your market is. But, with a radio show, you want to really niche it tight.

2. **Do your homework**. In other words, do your research. I knew I wanted to go out and reach women like me, the Boomer women. So, I listened to other shows that had the same or similar message. I listened to them. I learned from them. I learned what I liked, and didn't like, and that's what you want to do.

3. **Pick your show name and begin to create and format it**. How long will your show be and how often will you do it? Will you deliver the content or will you do like I do and interview experts? What will your show be about? Is it going to be the same as your business, or is it going to be a little bit different? That's ok if it is. For example, if you are an agent for Century 21 Real Estate but your show might be named something different. Like Your First Home talk radio show – where you get the insider secrets to purchasing your first home and how to maintain it once you buy it. This is a fantastic

way to attract new customers, generate leads and build your sales funnel without you directly having to contact anyone. Remember your listeners will also find you and if they like your message they'll also share you with their family and friends. Another quick example, if you are a minister you might want to make your message, or radio show more tailored to you not the church. You could talk about the different charities or organizations you're passionate about. If you've written a book, you can discuss it then you can promote the church as the sponsor and feed people back to the church.

Now it's time to begin to create and format your show. Figure out how long you want your show to be. Do you want a twenty minute show, a ten minute tip type show, or do you want to do interviews and make it thirty minutes to an hour? The average commute is twenty minutes, so the shorter the show, the more successful your show will be. If you can do a show in twenty minutes, it would be ideal because most people have reached their destination within twenty minutes. If you want to stretch it, you can go to thirty minutes.

4. **Get your tools**. What tools do you need to produce your show? You are going to need: a telephone, a headset with a microphone, **or** a standalone microphone, recording equipment, and editing software so you can edit out all the 'ums' and 'you knows'.

5. **Record your first show**. Once you've created it and formatted it then you are going to record and edit it.

6. **Upload and post it** in ITunes, other directories and your current web site.

7. **Get the word out!** Send out press releases and announcements saying "My show is up; I've launched it." Let others enjoy hearing your message.

"Follow your instincts.

That's where true wisdom manifests itself."

Oprah

HOW TO IDENTIFY YOUR TARGET MARKET

What makes a target market or "niche?" By definition, a niche is a particular area that is in need of a product or service that isn't being fulfilled by the mainstream market. For example: If you live in a town where there are thousands of area residents but no store for twenty miles, a general store will do exceptionally well. If you try to fit a general store into the middle of a city, you'll find business really doesn't thrive because people have too many options. The same is true with the Internet. This is what finding a niche is about.

Bringing customer and business together is important to any market. No matter what you plan to offer in your podcast, you will run into obstacles if you cannot tap into a strong listener base. When you broadcast information online that customers do not need or can easily get from other podcasts, your show is bound to fail.

Finding a niche makes your company stand out. If you find a niche that has little to no competition, you are far more likely to become a success. But keep in mind that the lack of competition could also mean that there isn't a market for it. Therefore it's extremely important that you do your market research before you entrench yourself within a particular niche, regardless of the competition level.

Don't try to be Wal-Mart! I once heard from an online podcaster, Kelly McCausey, explain what that means. She said, in short, you can't be everything to everybody and you can't be for everyone. You need to zoom in on your target market and offer a solution to their problems and needs. They will come to you because they trust you and they feel special because you are talking to them. When they hear your podcast, they will say this is the show for me; this is MY show, because she/he is addressing my needs. When you try to throw in something else for another audience, it confuses your listeners and they don't know to whom you are talking.

Others, outside your niche, may find you, like what you're saying and become a listener too! After starting Women Power, I received an email from a listener, Sarah Zeldman. She had found my show through iTunes and even though my target audience was "boomer" women in their 40's and above, she was in her early thirties and loved the show. She recommends it to all her thirty something friends. So even if you focus on a target market, others will find you if what you are saying resonates with them.

When it comes to the Internet, the stakes are raised. With competition located on all corners of the globe, you need to make sure your podcast is competitive throughout. By searching for smaller segments of much larger markets, you can easily develop and promote a podcast that will exclusively serve a targeted customer base.

Finding your niche is easier than you think. Make a list of your favorite hobbies or activities. No matter what the hobby, put it on the list—sewing, computer games, reading, cooking, baking, etc. State those hobbies that you feel you are exceptionally good at. Use this list to come up with podcast ideas.

I think one of the things that was difficult for me at first was the fact that everybody wasn't going to listen to my show! It wasn't for everybody. My show was for women over forty. So people who were not interested in going for their dreams and visions and how they can recreate their lives after 40 weren't coming to my show.

You need to zoom in and have a laser focus on:

- Who you are delivering your content to.
- Who will want the products and services you offer.
- Who are you going to attract.

Once you really, really zoom in, you will be able to spend your time marketing to the right people instead of wasting your time, money, and energy delivering your message to the wrong audience.

Most people want to make some income from their show. They want to sell products and services from their show. In creating your show and thinking about the show you want, sometimes it may not be the show that you need to have. Ask yourself, “What kind of show would help meet my personal and professional goals?”

There are thousands of possible ideas. As long as you have a hobby and a bit of creativity, you can turn your favorite pastime into a thriving business. Remember to be open to trying different spins on your hobby. If you narrow your idea down and find that there are tons of competing businesses, you will need to come up with a suitable option that sticks with your interests while matching a customer's requirements.

"My theory is I'm not doing anything special.
The thing I've learned, from listening to a mentor of mine,
Jerry Clark, if you don't A-S-K, ask you won't G-E-T, get."

Raven Blair Davis

SECURING GUESTS

When you're thinking about guests, you want to find experts on your topic. Start making a list of at least ten top people that you want to interview. Make sure at least one is pretty well known so you can start your show with a bang!

Remember, if you want to monetize your podcast, one way to do that is to obtain sponsors and they want to see big names!

Think of the perfect guest for your show and audience. Don't just go after someone famous who doesn't have anything to do with your niche. Once you get the first guest, ask them for a referral. Just ask, *"Who do you know that would be open to being a guest on my show?"*

Never pay guests for their appearance! There are too many people out there that want exposure. They're already selling tons of whatever but they still want exposure. They still want to get plugged into someone else's audience, someone that doesn't know them. So you do not have to pay for guests. Don't let anyone even take you there.

When finding your experts, be sure to provide them with enough information so they will want to do your show. Let them know they are going to get an MP3 or a CD of the show. Everybody wants a copy to put on their media page or to give away to their list. So *always, always* offer them a copy of the recording.

You also want to get a guest agreement.

Try to arrange for a 10 minute "get to know you" conversation once they agree to be your guest and before your interview. I did one interview where I did not talk to the person until the day of the interview. The interview was alright to everybody else but to me the connection was just not there.

"Desire creates the power."

Raymond Holliwell

Branding

One of the most important things to do when starting your podcast is to BRAND it. This should be done before you market or promote your podcast. Branding your podcast will send a consistent message to your audience and establish your image and purpose.

If you want to differentiate your podcast from others, you need to take the time to plan your branding before you ever publish your first podcast.

This includes:

- Selecting a Name for your podcast
- Securing a Domain Name
- Create a Logo
- Music, Sound Effects
- Marketing

The first step is to identify your theme or writing your podcast description. Be sure that it explains the purpose of your show and the theme of your podcast. The description should only be two to three sentences long.

Step Two is selecting a name. The name of your podcast should reflect the content that you are delivering. For example, for *Women Power Radio*, my content is based on the theme of empowering boomer women to achieve their dreams. It's also a good idea to make sure the name you choose is available as a domain name. It should be easy to remember AND type.

Which leads to Step Three, secure the domain name for your podcast. This is extremely important because interested listeners and inquisitive searchers will be able to find your podcast in Search engines such as Google, Yahoo!, MSN and others.

Next, you need to create a logo. Probably the most seen and easily distributed representative of your podcast is your logo. I t can accompany press releases, be used as a link to your site, for advertising purposes, and give potential audiences a glimpse at what you and your podcast are all about even before listening to your show.

Logos are often the first impression of your podcast. This makes it very important. Your logo should be friendly to your targeted market as well as sized appropriately. Make sure that it is the customary size and dimension for logos. To unify the visual branding it should incorporate the colors of your website or blog.

You can outsource logo design to a freelance graphic designer or firm or design your own using software on your computer. If your company already has a logo, your podcast logo should be very similar or even a variation of the corporate logo.

Then you are on to the music and sound effects. This includes the music that heralds segments, music beds underneath segments, and closing music. The music selected can be based upon a theme and vary throughout the podcast. This is known as theme and variation.

For instance, the intro music, which is also the music that is most associated with your podcast, is the main theme that the remaining music revolves around. The closing music should nearly mirror the intro music with a more subdued variation, finishing with a cadence or fading out to end the show.

Sound effects can be interspersed throughout the show while you are speaking, or can be nestled into the musical theme and variations. When selecting sound effects, make sure that they are appropriate to your show and are used sporadically to compliment your podcast.

There are a few options for acquiring music and sound effects. You can purchase royalty-free music and sound effects, hire a composer to create custom work for your podcast, or compose your own music.

It is vitally important to brand all aspects of your podcast. When inspiration strikes, have a good brainstorm and jot down as many ideas about your podcast vision as possible and use the results to brand your podcast.

Marketing is all about building relationships. You build relationships with your potential clients through your podcast. They hear from you and your guest experts on your podcast.

Do you realize by being a "host" you are automatically considered an expert by association? Think about how much expert status you give to your favorite talk show host or even game show host! Now your podcast goes out on itunes as well as the internet and everybody in the world can hear it!

That's a nice passive way of marketing. It's passive because you don't have to do anything except your initial podcast. Your listeners will start talking about it and soon your show is all over blogs and social networks. It's all increasing identity awareness and your memorability.

PODCASTING TO INCREASE YOUR SEARCH ENGINE RANKING

You can you use your audio, which you already created, and leverage it to bring more hits to your website and have more people find you. It's called RSS feed or keyword syndication. If you have ever seen a television program, if you watch the television program today or tonight, chances are it was a repeat. Maybe it was one of the older shows like Seinfeld or Andy Griffith. These shows are in syndication. This means they were recorded once but now they are being duplicated and replayed all over the world in other places at other times. So it's getting a lot more visibility.

You can tape recordings of your radio shows and put them on RSS feed. It's just a different kind of webpage - no need to freak out! There are programs that create the RSS feed for you and it's not any different than filling out a form and filling in the blanks. That's how easy it is to do a podcast. Because you already have recordings and you already know how to upload them to the Internet. You have the hardest part already taken care of. It would be a hop, skip and a jump for you to start podcasting. It wouldn't cost you a red cent and it will increase your search engine ranking.

Once you take your audio and put it on this RSS feed, you now have a link and address (URL). You've got a name for your radio show but now you have something called the XML feed. It is the address where people can find your RSS feed.

Why the RSS is feed so important? With this special kind of webpage people can actually subscribe to the webpage. When people want to come to listen to your radio show, they have to bookmark your site and come back to it; it doesn't come to them. Now you might be able to send them an email letting them know what that is, but they have to remember to come back to your website in order to enjoy your media. With RSS feed, RSS pages have their own browsers RSS feed also helps you keep listeners. It allows the people who like to listen to you to actually subscribe to your podcast. When they subscribe to it with an RSS reader, their browser or RSS reader will actually go at certain intervals of every six to twelve hours and check your RSS feed to see if you have posted anything new on it. If you have, then it goes back and tells your listener, "Hey she's got a new show, let me show it to you!" And it shows up in the RSS reader.

So this makes it much easier for listeners to pay attention to and track the audio that they want to continue to listen to and they don't have to remember when it is because whenever a new show goes up, ding, ding, ding, it shows up on their computer. It is a beautiful, beautiful thing for those of us who want other people to be listening to us. So number one, your listeners can subscribe to you and number two, you can syndicate, you can reprint or republish your podcast, your audio, and text along with it on tons of other websites.

Now it's time to start thinking about some winning Keywords.

Search engine ranking depends on the search engine robot. However, search engines don't read audio and video. Search engines read words. Therefore, it's incredibly important that the best podcasts have the text that will go with it in a blog.

Think of a podcast as a very well-written blog that also has a link to your audio or video in it. That way you get the best of both worlds. A lot of people think, "Well I'd like to blog but I don't have any content." You DO have content! Every time you do a show do an overview of the interview that you did or what the show was about utilizing keywords that other people are searching for. You don't have to do an exact translation or transcription of it just the written summary.

We all do keywords backwards. For example, I might say my keywords for *Women Power Talk Radio* are – women, power, talk, radio. That's not necessarily true. What you need to do is find words that other people are already searching for. Most of the time, people will not find you because they're searching for you. Better keywords for *Women Power Talk Radio* would be - empowerment, women's talk show, women over forty, women's support, and boomer women.

People will find you because they're searching for something else and you will stumble across their path via the search engine. So you need to find out what your target clientele, your target market is searching for. What are the words they're typing into Google in the little search box? And then you need to start talking about those subjects. You need to start doing shows that involve that information. So when people do a Google search, your show or website shows up and they find. The end result is new listeners, who are targeted, potential customers, for you!

"Whoever renders service to many puts himself in line for greatness – great wealth, great return, great satisfaction, great reputation, and great joy."

Jim Rohn

MONETIZE YOUR PODCAST

Who Says You Can't Make Money From Your Podcast or Radio Show?

Even if you are brand new in your business and no one knows who you are, you can and should be monetizing your show as quickly as possible.

You can do your first 3 to 5 shows free if you feel you need to have something to show before charging, then after that think $$$$$$ signs.

I learned from my mentor, Alex Mandossian, to place value on your time, your content, and your show. Alex says to ask yourself before doing each show, "How will I monetize today from this interview or this show?"

Remember your show is your business or an extension of your current business. This is not vanity radio you're doing, this is reality radio with quality content that your listeners enjoy and depend upon. This is also your business so have a strategic workable plan. A great lady by the name of Mary Kay Ash is known for saying, "To be successful in business -you have to plan your work and work your plan."

With that in mind, to assist you in getting started in the right direction, I've listed a few ways to create and generate income for your show. Choose the option that feels right to you, put them into immediate action and make it happen....you can do it!

Below are nine creative ways I've found to generate income as a talk show host and you can too!

1. Create products, books, audio series, or reports from the content in your podcast

2. Create audio recordings per show and sell either transcript or show notes with it. (Sell mp3 or CD version of audio)

3. Charge a fee for business owners/ authors/coaches etc. to be interviewed on your show

4. Hire yourself out as a host on live virtual book tours for authors

5. Train, coach and mentor business owners and fortune 500 companies in creating their own radio show/podcast for their business.

6. Hire yourself out as a Master or Mistress of Ceremonies for events.

7. Speak at schools, colleges, chambers of commerce, seminars and events about why they should be podcasting

8. Promote you own products and services on your show

9. Form Joint Venture alliances with your guests

Yes, a podcast can make you money. Bottom line: don't limit your thinking that your podcast is only an informative and entertaining resource used for website owners. Think of your podcast/radio show as an extension of your current or existing business. Or if you're like me it is your business so don't treat it like a hobby, treat it like a business and it will pay you like a business.

After all, we're talking about using the internet; so of course, money making opportunities aren't far behind the idea. Here are some additional ways in which a podcast can bring you a little- or maybe a lot- of extra cash:

1. **Advertisements:** Think of the radios and television stations. How do they make their money? Through use of commercial advertisements. Companies pay the stations to air their commercials during a popular program. Podcasts are no different in that sense. Advertisements can be placed within your own programs and you can profit from it. This can also be done by providing advertisements on the podcast's blog as well. This gets the companies' ad noticed and then both of you earn a profit.

2. **Podcast for pay:** If you're providing a high quality program that gives a unique perspective on a topic; listeners will pay to download the podcast. Set a fee for your podcast programs that you feel is worth your time and effort put into creating it. Don't set it too high, if

you're just starting out, as this will help you build a rapport with your listeners. Once it becomes more popular, you can start charging more.

3. **Donations:** Some podcasters make their money from donations. The podcast is generally offered for free and a PayPal button is placed on their site or blog allowing satisfied listeners to donate a few dollars to the podcasters to help keep the show running. The more people that donate to your program; the more profits that can be made for putting back into the show and for adding to your income.

Even though little money is put into creating and publishing a podcast program, there's no reason why you shouldn't make money from this medium. Earn some extra cash to pay for the costs you do put into it and for the time you put forth to bring informative content for your listeners.

"If you are ready to get started, say I'm ready and if you are ready to truly, truly put the commitment into getting your own show going, then I want you to get excited starting right now, at this point."

RAVEN BLAIR DAVIS

Preparing to Launch

The Do's and Don'ts of Podcasting

- ✓ DO prepare for your first show! Make sure you have prepared your guests by talking to them before the show and letting them know what to expect. Share the questions you will ask or topics you will discuss on the show. Coach them on how to be a great guest!

- ✓ DO be organized! Know what you will be talking about and how long it will take to cover your topic. Make an outline. Write out your bullet points.

- ✓ DO mute your call waiting! On most phone services, pressing *70 will turn off call waiting. It may seem like a small thing, but that little beep is very hard to edit out and annoying to live listeners.

- ✓ DON'T wait until the last minute to find guests! Your calendar should be booked as far in advance as possible but minimum of a week before the show.

- ✓ DON'T be afraid to stop your guest and ask them to speak louder or clearer. Sometimes people talk quieter or faster when they are nervous. Your live listeners need to hear clearly what is being said and, here again; it is very difficult to edit your recording to adjust for volume or clarity.

Launch Preparation

- ✓ Be sure your content and or guests are ready.
- ✓ Once you've prepared record and edit your first show.
- ✓ Promote your show to your email list, Facebook, Twitter, MySpace, LinkedIn, etc.
- ✓ Record or prepare your commercial and links to promote your product or service during your show.
- ✓ Obtain paid sponsors for your show.

Launching your show is the easy part! There are some insider secrets and skills you'll need to master in order to stand out of the crowd. You need to be a great tele-connector. Connect with people in a very sincere and authentic way that says you can trust me … I am relaxed on your show… I want to give you something I never shared with anyone else. When your guest feels like this you'll end up with an incredible interview that you'll be proud to broadcast.

The 5 P's of a Successful Talk Show

Learn to master the art of what I call the 5 P's. It will truly elevate your business quickly.

1. Passion for what you're doing …passion for your show…your topic…your market. Your listeners should hear and feel your passion. Your voice needs to express that you love what you do and believe it.

2. Purpose. Know your purpose for your show. Be clear and consistent. Do not give your listeners mixed messages. Remember to be true to yourself, your purpose, and your audience.

3. Personality. We all have it. I say let it shine like the sun! Don't be afraid to let your personality out …don't be an old stick in the mud and be too professional. Personality sells which means you will attract tons of listeners who will eventually be customers and clients.

4. Prepare for your show at all times. Be ready for the guest. Have your questions and their bio. Check your volume, have your recording line ready, and, before the show, take the time to prepare your guest with what they need and what you expect from them so this can be a successful show for both of you.

5. Persistence and Patience. Never give up. If at first you don't succeed, try, try again. Good things come to those who wait. You'll get that dream interview if you just don't give up. You will sell more books, get more speaking engagements, and attract advertiser and sponsors if you don't give up.

Master Going from Good to Great

Keeping your listeners first is the sign of a great host. It's not about you. Give your listeners what they want and what they need. Keep in mind that your show is not about you it's about your listeners. Your show is to assist them with reaching their goals and helping them solve their problem or challenge. Your purpose is to give them the answers they need to encourage, inspire, and uplift them to move forward in their personal, business, or financial situation.

A great talk show host will make her guest feel special because they are....that is why they are on your show. Always edify them. Give them the opportunity to talk about their product or service before they leave. Make them feel like being on your show was one of the best experiences they have had and would love to come back at any time.

A great radio host is creative and thinks out the box to make that interview special. The day before I interviewed Jack Canfield a friend of mine shared with me that it was his birthday. As soon as I got off the phone, I immediately went into creative mode and I decided to download Stevie Wonders Happy Birthday 2u song on Utube. At the end of the interview, live on air, I said, "Jack, before we go I heard today is your birthday and someone wants to say happy birthday to you. "Then I played about 1 minute of Stevie's song. Jack laughed and thanked me. When we were off the air, I asked him if he would write a testimonial and he said gladly. Not only did he write me an incredible testimonial, he copied me on a letter he wrote to Mark Victor Hansen saying you have got to be on her show. So being creative is definitely a good thing.

Be creative and leave your guest with an enjoyable and memorable experience on your show. They will not only tell their friends and business associates that they should consider being a guest too; they will also be willing to give you a testimonial or endorsement for either your show or your future products. How important are testimonials? I strongly feel that they are extremely important and very rewarding.

Testimonials will attract other experts as guests and will help you stand out as an expert yourself in the radio/podcast industry which means more opportunities to profit from your show or from being a talk show host. Having testimonials also adds credibility and will help make your potential customers and clients feel the trust they need to move forward and purchase your products and services.

Here are a few of the testimonials I have on my website from top experts and celebrities. I can truly say from the heart that they have assisted me tremendously in growing my career as a talk show host.

"I have appeared on more than 800 radio interview shows in the past 20 years, and my time with Raven Blair Davis on her show "Careers from the Kitchen Table" was one of the most enjoyable ever. She is a rare combination of dynamic, spontaneous and fun, as well as thoroughly prepared, deeply insightful and a great listener who responds with great follow-up questions as well as her own experiences in a way that moves the conversation forward without stealing the focus. I would highly recommend being on her show to anyone who is serious about getting your message out to more people--and enjoying the process at the same time."

Jack Canfield
America's #1 Success Coach
www.JackCanfield.com

"Over the course of my yeas as an actress and these last three years as a published writer, I've done interviews for all kinds of media, as well as in-person talks with Travis Smiley, Larry King and many others. I absolutely enjoyed my time with Raven Blair Davis. Raven's questions were well though, insightful and there was even time for laughter. The interview laid out the silk road and the bumpy road for anyone ready to take the trip of reaching for a dream, no matter what age. She's the Best!! Thanks Raven!... Best Wishes"

Denise Nicholas
Acclaimed Actress

"Aloha this is Wally Amos at Chip and Cookie.com – Listening to Raven Blair Davis helps you connect to the real you. Doing her show was one of my best interviews. Do yourself a favor and listen to Raven Blair Davis, you'll enjoy her kitchen table talk. You will be glad you did! Alo-ha!!!!"

Wally Amos
Cookie Man and Literacy Advocate
www.ChipandCookie.com

"Do you want a talk show that is fresh and inspiring? This is the Lady!

Raven has such a unique way of making learning fun and interesting both for her listeners and those participating in her radio show. S he is definitely a lady to pay attention to for powerful and practical tools for your career from the kitchen table and beyond. Raven has a great sensitivity as an interviewer. She knows the right questions to ask to get to the heart of a matter and find the wisdom that will benefit her listeners in a powerful way."

Douglas Vermeeren

www.DouglasVermeeren.com
Creator of THE OPUS www.TheOpusMovie.com and the upcoming TV SHOW Powerful Possibilities www.MMPWMovies.com

"Destiny is not a matter of chance, it is a matter of choice, it is not a thing to be waited for, it is a thing to be achieved."

William Jennings Bryant

TIPS FROM THE PROS

Here are a few tips from the pros that I received from an interview I did for a soon to be release audio series called Kitchen Table Radio "Tips from the Pros" where I interviewed over twenty mentors I've admired and learned from both in the past and in the present.

Remember.....You too can become a GREAT TALK SHOW HOST and have a successful and profitable show. If you *Think* the thoughts and claim the *Beliefs* of other great talk show host. Claim the thoughts and beliefs of the "Pros" AS YOUR OWN....starting today!

Dr. Tony Marino is one of the podcasting pioneers. He specializes in creating interactive websites that deliver high quality audio and video content that is combined with great copywriting to tell a compelling story that communicates your important message.

- **Be Open to Everything and Closed to Nothing.** Develop a relationship first. Stack the deck in your favor. Then when you write the contract or offer a service you already know you can help the potential client.
- **When broadcasting, always talk to ONE person**. Even though you may have thousands listening each person must feel like you are speaking directly to them.

- **Understand your core market.** Your show is not about YOU – it's about your audience. It's about what your audience wants.

- **Build your list in traditional ways.** Drive traffic to your website, submit to podcast directories, article submission, and squeeze pages. Give away A LOT when building your list. Create an "inner circle." People want to belong and be a part of a community.

- **Make yourself the best YOU can be.** Set goals and make a plan to work toward them. But be flexible with yourself and your goals. Don't get discouraged if you don't meet a goal. Re-evaluate and continue. Remember you are unique. The only wrong way to do your show is to not prepare.

- **Achieve a goal – solve a problem – satisfy a need.** Getting on AM radio is simple. Ask. Study the demographics and format of the station and then call them and tell them you want to do a show. Then you just have to find an available time slot and pay for the time.

- **Secure sponsors and advertisers.** Never discount your rate. You can "give" extra spots but never discount your rate. You are not selling price – you are selling value.

Jayne Kennedy Overton is an acclaimed actress, model and sportscaster. Jayne was crowned Miss Ohio USA 1970 (she was the first African American woman to win the title), and was one of the 10 semi-finalists in the 1970 Miss USA pageant. During the 1970s, she had over 10 notable TV guest appearances and roles in seven movies. In 1978, she was one of the first women to infiltrate the male-dominated world of sports announcing with a role on The NFL Today.

- **Bring out the personality of the people you interview.** Establishing relationships is key in order to have access to information and people. It has to be beneficial to both.

- **The most important part of doing an interview is knowing your subject matter.** Research the people you will be interviewing.

- **Listening is a key skill.** When you don't listen to the answers to questions, the interviewee feels like they are not being engaged. You need to actually carry on a conversation and that's when you really get some gems. It is critically important to make sure your interview subject is comfortable. They should be comfortable with the host as a person and your ability to speak freely; they also need to be comfortable in their seat and their environment.

- **Always be prepared**. You never know how an interview is going to go so always be prepared to put your best foot forward.
- **Don't be afraid to be controversial.**
- **Don't be afraid to ask the question.**
- **Creative marketing is a must!**
- **Don't stay with the status quo.**
- **Number 1 is to *earn Respect* and *keep Respect.***
- **Number 2 is Be Loyal.**
- **Be respectful of your interviewee.** Don't answer your cell phone, don't step on their lines, or answer their questions. This is their time and you should be respectful of it. The most important thing you can do is be sincere.

Doug Vermeeren is the creator of the best selling inspirational film, "The Opus." The author of a multitude of books and articles, he is currently published in more than 22 languages worldwide. Doug is one of the top business and personal success speakers in the world. An amazing motivator who has conducted 10 years of extensive research into the lives of more than 400 of the world's top achievers. He understands what top achievers know and can help you get to your goals instantly.

- **When interviewing, be yourself.**
- **Be very conversational.**
- **Don't try to lead the interviewee down a certain path.**
- **Be very open and pliable.**
- **Ask people around you that you know, "Who do you think I should talk to?"** Everyone knows someone and can introduce you.
- **If you know someone you want to interview**, send them email or letter. Don't be shy. Ask for the interview.

- **Be clear with your intentions** about the interview and the benefits to the interviewee.

- **Give the interviewee the opportunity to share** what they want to get across.

- **Look for positive examples** and watch what they do, i.e., Larry King, Oprah, etc.

- **After an interview or speaking engagement**, talk to people and ask what they want to know or what questions they have. Then always be on the lookout for the answer.

- **Search for a person's principles** and examples from their life that illustrate the principle.

- **Content is number one** – people won't listen if they aren't getting any information.

- **Be focused.** You need to be focused so your listeners know what they are getting.

- **Create a perception of being an expert in your market.**

- **Be clear about how much time you need and honor it.**

- **Speak from the heart. Be authentic.**

Ending Thoughts

Podcasts are wonderful resources anyone can use for tutorials, music demos, educational training, newsletters and much, much more. This audio opportunity grows more each day.

Add a blog or website to your podcast program, so that people can see notes or view a whole transcript of the program as well as listen to the audio content. This will help you make the most of all the internet media outlets available for your business.

Get on the bandwagon and profit from this internet marketing tool and increase your sales or earn some extra cash. Podcasting will be around for a long time, so don't be left behind in the dust that your competitors could leave you in.

Bottom line, it's your time to shine my friend. So, why not do it with your own internet radio talk show or podcast and begin to ***Podcast Your Passion or Business to Profits*** and start growing your business exponentially. Get your message out, promote your business anytime you want for "free," attract new customers, retain your current ones, sell more books, and get more speaking engagements.

Become the star you are because there is power in your voice.

Dreams Do Come True!

Having my radio shows has truly changed my life. I have risen from being a telemarketer part time from home making $200 a week to now having a thriving successful home base business. And the best part, I now help many others with a burning desire and strong passion just like "you" to learn how to get their message out around the world and make a profit from it.

I show them how to get top experts to grant them an interview just like I've done. In the past three years, I've had the pleasure of interviewing award winning authors, celebrities and great mentors and masters like Loral Langemeier, John Asaraff, Montel Williams, Lisa Nicholas, Fran Drescher, Lindsay Wagner, Wally Amos and many other amazing people who I had only read about.

People I had listened to on the radio and bought their songs or motivational audios. People I've seen at seminars, watched on TV and in movies. Now, not only have I interviewed them, I've become close friends with some and others have assisted me in creating products. I've become Joint Venture partners with many of them. I've learned from my good friend and mentor, Greg Norman, to "Act as if and to always "Expect a Miracle."

I'd like to share a moment in time that I hope will paint a clearer picture of the true power of podcasting and what having a voice with a strong and sincere message can do for you. It can open many doors and opportunities to you because you now are not only an expert in your industry but part of the media.

It was spring of 2007; I took an unexpected trip to Los Angeles to attend a one day "free" seminar Mark Victor Hansen was presenting. I always wanted to meet him and this was an opportunity to learn from one of the best. I felt a strong urge that I could not shake that I should attend. So I put a plan in motion and called my friend Qarlah (Carla) Carter, aka Qarlah Prince. She of course insisted I stay with her and I decided to stay an entire week since it was my very first time going to Los Angeles which was a place I always dreamed about.

On my last day there, I made a phone call in hopes of having lunch with a new friend ...little did I know I was about to have a day, a moment that I would never forget. That is the day I sat in Claudette Robinson's (formerly The first lady of Motown) home as she gave me the grand tour - sharing photos of her and Smokey back during the Motown days. I got to see a napkin Smokey wrote one of his first songs on. I saw a lot of their memorabilia placed throughout her home. I had a chance to meet Tamala, their daughter, and Berry, their son, as well as her beautiful granddaughter, Lyric, who has an absolutely b-e-a-u-t-i-f-u-l voice. At the end of the interview, she was sweet enough to sing, "You are My Sunshine" and dedicated it to my grandson, Christian. Oh, I forgot to include that part I took my mp3 player with me to LA so that I would have it just in case Qarlah introduced me to someone that I felt would be interesting to interview for my show. I am so glad I took it with me because I'll always have that moment in time on recording since Claudette did agree to me doing a short teaser interview to take back and share with the Women Power listeners. WOW - what a moment! One I'll never forget and will always be grateful for. Her friendship and her kindness allowing me, someone who had just begun her show just a few months before, that exciting day meet her and her family. Someone she briefly met through an email from her good friend and now mine Jayne Kennedy that simply said *"Raven would like to interview you on her show Women Power, Claudette, here is her email if you're interested. "*

I had at that point never interviewed Claudette but had spoken many times over the telephone. During those calls she never asked me how long I had my show or how many listeners I had. We just connected very well and through that a friendship developed.
When I visited Los Angeles and called to say hello and to see if it would be possible to maybe have lunch, she graciously invited me to come by. I had the unbelievable opportunity to visit her and experience that one of many memorable moments.

You will have moments like that too. If you would like to hear that interview and share that moment with me please email me via raven@womenpower-radio.com.

Yes, dreams do come true and for me that is just one of many - too many to share in this one book. For me, having my podcast/radio shows and being a talk show host has been a true blessing as well an incredible and amazing journey. I now know and can appreciate from the heart, first hand exactly what one of my favorite mentors, Zig Ziggler, meant when he said, *"You will get all you want in life if you help enough other people get what they want."*

What a wonderful, rewarding feeling it is to receive so many emails from my listeners, not only in the U.S. but Canada, Europe, Australia and beyond, telling me how listening to one of my shows has helped them get through a difficult situation, or has given them hope during a time they had given up. There is so much pleasure in knowing you have helped someone. It truly makes you smile not just on the outside but in the inside too. You can't get better than that!

In closing I'd like to share with you what I feel are the secrets to podcasting your business for profitable results. Follow these and all the other golden nuggets shared throughout this book and you will not only have a very rewarding and successful podcast/radio show but you'll have one that makes you money over and over again.

1. Set up your podcast from the start to be a winning success and remember it's not about you it's about your audience.

2. Practice the Powerful P's of a talk show host and keep them visible until you know them by heart.

3. Treat your show like a business and not a hobby at all times! I learned from one of my mentors, Alex Mandossian, to always ask yourself *how will I make money from my show today/this week/ this month.*

4. Don't settle for being just a good talk show host ...... when you can be “great."

5. Remember content is "King and Queen" so give your best right from the start-don't hold back.

6. If you plan on interviewing guests, make your dream interview list and then "ask.”

7. Start your day out with a plan and work it. Don't get off track, stay laser focused until you reach your goal, be consistent with your show goals.

8. When in doubt, do like my friend, Greg Norman, says *"Act as If".* Walk the walk, talk the talk and expect miracles along the journey. Believe, take the necessary action steps to make it happen and expect only the best.

9. Market your business both online and offline, get in the mix -use social media, meet up groups etc.

10. Surround yourself with winners not losers. Positive people who can help you along your journey and in turn offer them assistance too.

11. Don't try to do everything yourself. Make a list of what you need and form a team of people who can assist you. Read *Tim Ferris' book "Four Hour Work Week".* Like me I bet you will be glad you did.

12. My final tip is if you want to do it faster rather than slower.....get a mentor or master to coach you along the way. Someone that has been there and done that. They can keep you from making a lot of unnecessary mistakes and can make sure you start out the way you want to end up *Successfully Broadcasting Your Passion To Profits.*

    In case you haven't figured it out yet that ....that would be me. Yes I am here to take you from this point all the way through to launching your winning, rewarding and profitable show.

ARE YOU READY TO GET STARTED?

Are you ready to begin to broadcast your passion to profits?

I'd like to invite you to come and join me, Raven Blair Davis, executive producer and host of 3 successful radio talk shows:
Women Power
Mentoring from MLM Divas Live!
Careers From The Kitchen Table

I will share my talk show host secrets during a 10 hour audio series from my exclusive Kitchen Table Radio Personal Broadcast Course.

You Will Get The Exact Steps To Go From Ground Zero to Launching Your First Show!

Now you can get my easy to follow, step-by-step formula for creating and launching your radio show on less than a shoestring budget.

You'll discover the real secrets to:

- Just how easy it really is to create and launch your show without having to buy expensive equipment

- How being a talk show host can be a great platform for you and your business
- What type of format is best for you and how long your show really should be
- How to record, post and edit your show with ease
- The easiest way to create content for your show that will keep your listeners coming back for more
- How to get the guest of your dreams
- The fastest, easiest and simplest way to attract and build a worldwide audience
- When you should do a free vs. paid internet radio show or podcast
- How to make a profit from your show even when you're first beginning
- How to instantly get listed in itunes and over 50 other top podcast directories
- and much more...

I'll give you my winning scripts to help you land local and nationwide sponsors, as well as a copy of my personal email I sent that helped me land some of my top guests like acclaimed actress Jayne Kennedy, best-selling author Cynthia Kersey, former President Clinton diarist Janis F. Kearney, and many others.

To order today go to www.kitchentableradio.com

Whether You Want To Interview Celebrities, Business Owners or Simply Experts in Their Chosen Fields, Creating a Talk Show Is For You!

Here's What Students of the *Kitchen Table Radio Home Study Course* Had to Say!

"Raven was a wonderful friend and mentor, as I was struggling to do my share in learning. As I was often restricted in time I found that Raven was so incredibly patient and talented and always took the extra time to give me more info and another extra little nudge, to get me to where I needed to be."

"I'm so very excited to get my show launched in a few days; it was a pleasure to work with Raven. She really knows what she is doing, and she shares that great knowledge graciously. I strongly suggest you consider starting your own show, too and take advantage of her program. She is a pro and committed to the success of her students.
Thank you, Raven!"

Baerbel Froehlin, CHt./HypnoCoach, EFT-ADV
www.SmoothChanges.com

"You can have a life that you love, but it begins with knowing what you want and recognizing the vehicle to make it happen. I knew that it was time to get my message heard by many and the vehicle I chose was, Raven Blair Davis's Kitchen Table Radio course. The education and mentoring I received from her made producing and hosting a show realistic and doable. I jumped aboard the KTR movement and as a result I will debuted my show in June 2008 on LA Talk Radio formally known as BBS Talk Radio as the talk show host of my own live show 'Living Vivaciously'."

"By staying the course and utilizing her personal scripts and directives I was able to book well-known experts, I have already received sponsors and I exude the professionalism and language that's needed to be successful and create a loyal listenership. Her personal coaching sessions and commitment to my success helped me stay on task and be present and accountable to my own dream.

Every ingredient needed to go from good to great I experienced in the KTR course. So if you have a message that you want to share, I suggest you lay aside the "WAIT" and I recommend that you join the movement as a student of Kitchen Talk Radio, and allow Raven Blair Davis to make your dream realistic and doable. The time is now!!!"

Nekisha-Michelle, LMSW,

www.spajamaworks.com

"What started out as a great idea for our *Thriving Mother's Talk Radio Show* has blossomed into a very polished and fun show we are so proud to host. This happened in a few short months of meeting Raven Blair Davis.

One of the best decisions we made for our business was to jump in to her program: *Kitchen Talk Radio: Insider Secrets to Producing, Posting and Profiting from Your Own Talk Show.*

Raven's course took us by the hand and taught us how to set up and produce a successful show. From knowing who we were targeting, to getting the "ideal" guest, to editing the show, this course was the complete package. Raven's passion for helping people learn to broadcast what is most meaningful to them truly is an inspiration.

We invite you to check out our show and see what this course can do for you".

Mary McHenry and Susan Guiher
The Thriving Mother Talk Radio Show
www.thrivingmotherstalkradio.podomatic.com

Sign up now – go to www.kitchentableradio.com

Mention that you've read *"Broadcast Your Passion to Profits"* for a $200 discount!

Free Consultation

20 minutes – No Obligation

Call 800-431-0842 to schedule your time today!

Appendix 1 – Forms and Worksheets

Script out your interview opening comments:

Example:

Welcome to (WPR) Women Power Talk Radio, the show that's designed with the boomer women in mind and the men who love them. I'm your host, Raven Blair Davis. This show features unstoppable women of power. Today my guest is actress Bern Nadette Stanis formerly known as "Thelma" of the hit TV sitcom, Good Times. She is also the author of Situations 101 Relationships.

Today, I'm talking to Bern Nadette Stanis about dating, romance and relationships in our midlife. Bern Nadette Stanis, welcome to the show.

Who's Your Dream Guest?

Of all the people in the world, who would you most like to interview for your future show? List ten people:

____

____

____

____

Now it's your turn….. fill in the blanks:

"Welcome to ______________, I'm your host, _________. This show is ________. Today my guest is ______________, who is the _________. __________, welcome to the show."

Research your quest and note your opening comments:

____

____

____

____

____

Pick one of the above people. What 10 questions would you like to ask that person?

1. ____

2. ____

3. ____

4. ____

5. ____

6. ____

7. ____

8. ____

9. ____

10. ____

On the next page, you will see a sample newsletter.

WPRNews - July 9, 2009

In this issue:

- Women Power - Montel Williams
- Careers from the Kitchen Table - Wally Amos
- Raven's Celebrity Rave - Exciting changes!
- and much more!

Women Power Radio

Emmy Award Winning Talk Show Host, decorated former Navel Intelligence Officer, entrepreneur, motivational speaker and philanthropist.

Montel Williams is the author of New York Times bestselling book: "***Living Well Emotionally - Breakthrough To a Life of Happiness***", as well as inspirational memoirs "Climbing Higher and Mountain", "Get Out of My Way", and the co-author of the New York Times bestseller, "Bodychange."

Listen as Montel shares with Raven a chilling experience he had 10 years ago when he "thought" he was having a heart attack.

- You'll also hear Montel speak about the effect MS has on his body.
- The importance of not taking life for granted
- Montel talks about the day he got fired over the telephone and how he was forced to take control of the situation and create a new opportunity for himself
- Shares why we should to start paying attention (focus) to our physical and psychological well being ....starting today!

Click here to Listen right NOW!

Also be sure to listen to the end to hear what Montel announces exclusively on Women Power and why he's so excited about it.

To read Montel's story & listen weekly to his new radio show "**Montel Across America**," click **here**

Sample Press Release

Beacon Communications
P.O. Box 1577
Frederiksted, St. Croix 00841

www.beaconcommunications.com
Phone – 340.772.1111
Fax – 340.772.1112

FOR IMMEDIATE RELEASE – August 6, 2007

Contact: Laurie Christian
Office: 340.772.1111
Cellular: 340.772.1111

TALK SHOW HOST DEBUTS INTERNET RADIO CLASS

FOR BEGINNERS STRAIGHT FROM HER KITCHEN

St. Croix, USVI August 6, 2007 – Do you dream of one day hosting your own internet radio show and want to learn the basics? The recently launched "Kitchen Talk Radio: Insider Secrets to Producing, Posting and Profiting from Your Own Talk Show" classes might be exactly what you need.

This five-week series is the brainchild of Raven Blair Davis the executive producer and host of Women Power Radio. According to Davis, "I wanted to ..."

Women Power Radio is dedicated to ...

For further information, contact Raven Blair

Davis at 800-431-0842 or raven@womenpower-radio.com.

Appendix 2 Resources

- www.RoyaltyFreeMusic.com
- www.freeconferencecall.com
- www.Raven.AudioAcrobat.com
- www.audacity.com
- Wavepad editing www.wavepad.com
- Headset with microphone (I recommend Plantronics Brand, available at office supply stores and Radio Shack)
- Podomatic www.podomatic.com

Ravens Podcast links

- www.wprtalk.podomatic.com
- www.mlmdivas.podomatic.com
- www.careersfromthekitchentable.podomatic.com

Raven's Recommended Podcasts

A show for all you over 35 who want to get fit, have fun and feel free for the rest of your life. Why? Because it's never too late to get in shape and feel great. Wellness Wisdom expert Roslyn Franken shares personal insight from her own experiences as a cancer survivor who has also overcome battles with weight and self-image.

She also features informative and inspiring guests to help encourage and enlighten you on how to thrive in your life.

Receive a complimentary 25-minute "GET FIT-HAVE FUN-FEEL FREE NOW" 1-ON-1 Coaching session with Wellness Wisdom expert, Roslyn Franken. Call 1-877-852-5852 or send email to info@roslynfranken.com with GET FIT-HAVE FUN-FEEL FREE NOW in the subject line Roslyn Franken HowtoThriveafter35.podomatic.com

The Daring Dreamers Showcase

IDareYouRadio.com:

Inspiration and Resources for you
Daring Dreamers who say,
"Box? WHAT BOX?!?

The Daring Dreamers Showcase at IDareYouRadio.com:
Massive inspiration, powerful support and uncommon resources for you Daring Dreamers who say, "Box? WHAT box?!?"

GIVEAWAY: Change your Emotional Destiny! FREE ebook shows you how: Get I Dare You Get Free! at http://www.IDareYouRadio.com

CONTACT INFO:

Angela Treat Lyon: Lyon@IDareYouRadio.com

808-261-0941

"Heal Yourself Talk Radio" is a talk radio show designed to help those who are searching to obtain help in learning how to heal their mind, body and spirit.

Heal Yourself Talk Radio- Desire it, Believe it, Accept it, & Receive it.
Check out true life experiences, from Rebbekah to you, on each and every episode of her award winning Heal Yourself Talk Radio show.
http://www.healyourselftalk.com

Receive 40 Affirmation Wall papers for your computer plus more freebies by signing up for HYTR's newsletter today!
http://healyourselftalk.com/newsletter/newsletter-sign-up.html

Celebrating baby boomer women fifty and better: interviews with women who are changing lives, making a difference, and totally transforming the spirit and style of aging. Feisty Side of Fifty Radio. http://feistysideoffifty.com/feisty-side-of-fifty-radio/

Contact me for your free report: "The 5 Essential Keys to Finding Work After Fifty" Mary Eileen Williams's mew@feistysideoffifty.com

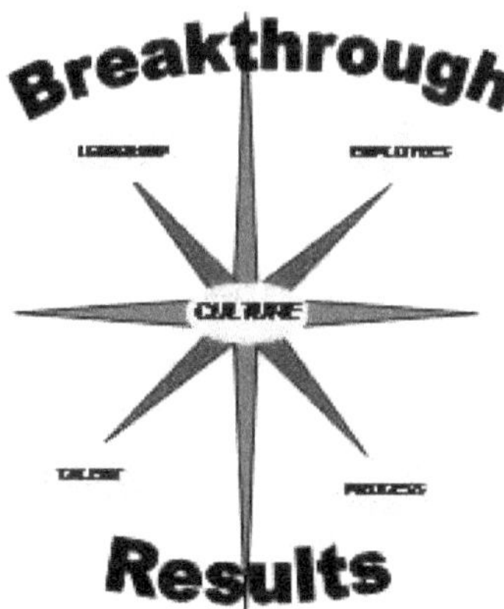

Safety Breakthrough Talk Radio is dedicated to helping people be better informed, so they can then make safer and healthier choices for themselves and their friends, families and colleagues at work.

Cathy's radio show can be found at http://cathyhansell.podOmatic.com.

For further information, contact Cathy Hansell at 888-609-6723 or at chansell@breakthroughresults.org or her website at www.breakthroughresults.org.

As an incentive to contact Cathy, she will offer free of charge an audiotape of Teen Driving Safety Best Practices.

COACH LORI SNYDER
www.coachlorisnyder.com

After Divorce Talk Radio with special segments of Sensational Singles with Coach Lori Snyder. This show will bring empowering and unstoppable confidence, ideas and success strategies in all areas of your life, mind, body and spirit, to the recently divorced and single crowd.

http://www.coachlorisnyder.com

Amazing Women Talk Radio: Women who are paying it forward, motivating, empowering, and inspiring women to be the very best they can be. Contact information: Tracey Doctor 281-240-2885 Contact us for a free ebook! traceydoctor@aol.com

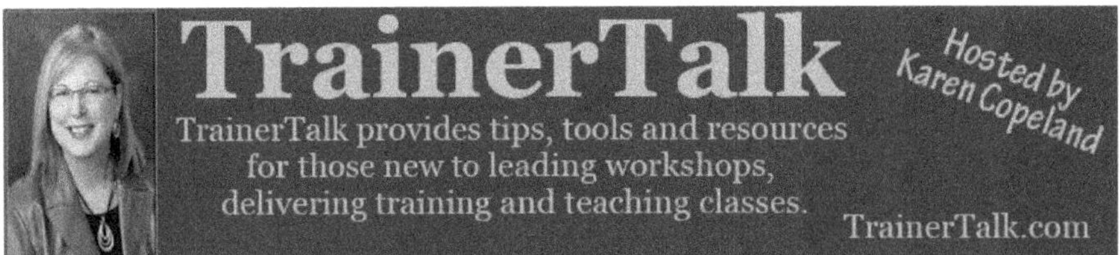

TrainerTalk, hosted by Karen Copeland, provides tips, tools and resources for those new to leading workshops, delivering training and teaching classes. Go to www.TrainerTalk.com/bonus for your free, downloadable, The Top 10

Training Problems and How to Overcome Them audio series. Contact info: Website: www.trainertalk.com Email: info@trainertalk.com

"Heroes at Home" Radio

"Ordinary Single Parents Achieving Extraordinary Things"

"Heroes at Home", hosted by Traci Campbell, celebrates single parents who have succeeded in achieving their personal dreams. Join us twice a month as we feature new and exceptional single parents who share their personal story of success from their heart.

Email Traci today and get your FREE audio introducing her popular C.H.A.M.P. concept (use code RAVEN785 on subject line and email Traci at info@heroesathomeradio.com)

Special Thanks to my loyal and dynamic partners for all your support in making *Broadcast Your Passion To Profits* another dream come true...I appreciate you!

Karen Salter www.Salterva.com Karen@Salterva.com

Click Here to Instantly Claim Your
14-Day Risk Free Test Drive
for Only $1

Regina Baker www.Wahmcart.com wahmcart@gmail.com

brochures
book design
catalogs
flyers
postcards
packaging
magazines
menus
newsletters
web updates

McCarthy's Business Services

Personalized Support Services For Your Business Success

Tracy McCarthy Tracy@McCarthysBusiness.com

Specializing in helping you become a Published Author!
Peggy Knudson Peggy@outstandingvirtualassistance.com

About The Author

Raven Blair Davis is a columnist, speaker, author, celebrity interviewer and executive producer as well as award winning talk show host of two global Internet Radio shows: Women Power Talk Radio and Mentoring from MLM Divas Live!

Raven, aka... The Talk Show Maven has over 25 years experience in telecommunications, tele-sales/telemarketing, customer service and management. She is known by friends, family, clients and associates as "The Telephone Diva" and feels you can do any job or create business over the phone, once you learn and master the art of tele-connecting. She is also live on 1320 WARL Am radio with her newest show, *Careers From The Kitchen Table*, and the author of Kitchen Table Radio - Home Study Course: How To Produce, Post and Profit from Your Own Radio Show."

Raven has been blessed to have interviewed powerful business owners, recording artists, and actors such as: Academy Award winning talk show host Montel Williams, international speaker Les Brown "The Motivator," acclaimed actress and one of the first female NFL sportscasters, Jayne Kennedy, actress Victoria Rowell (Young & The Restless), Fran Drescher (The Nanny), and Bern Nadette Stanis (Thelma from- Good Times), Lindsay Wagoner (The Bionic Woman), internet marketing guru Alex Mandossian, Dr Joe Joe Vitale, Lisa Nicholas and Jack Canfield from the inspirational movie "The Secret," financial strategists Loral Langemeier, bestselling author Cynthia Kearsey and that's just to name a few.

Ravens empowering radio network, *Women Power Radio*, was named 2008 and 2009 Best Top 100 Business podcast by Anita Campbell's Business Trends and she was named Universal 7 Radio Network's (1320 WARL AM) Talk Show Host of the Year for 2008 for her popular *Careers From The Kitchen Table* home business opportunity show.
www.careersfromthekitchentable.com

RAVENS PHOTO ALBUM:

Raven and her Mother Emily

I credit my mother with so much of my success – here's a poem she has written that shows you why:

Many Dreams

As distant as it may seem, life is full of many dreams. And if destiny had its way, we would look forward to a bright new day.

There would be no more sorrow, there would be no more pain, and no more misgivings that we could not explain.

So we dream of what we might have been, to bring us to a perfect end.

But someone is watching us from above and that someone fills our hearts with glorious love and what we find in him is so true. A big wide world, that's all brand new......field with gratitude, loves and delights laughter and sunshine...what a wonderful sight!

Life is full of many dreams and this is the dream I dreamed tonight.

Oh how sweet tomorrow will be a brand new world for you and me.

Poet: Emily M. Blair

Raven with Joan Rivers

Raven and Lisa Nicholas

Raven with Jeffrey Combs

Raven and Victoria Rowell

Raven and Qarlah

Raven and her husband, Larry

Raven, Mario Peebles and his family!

Larry, Jerry Clark & Raven

Raven with Vanessa Bell Callaway

"Until one is committed, there is hesitancy, the chance to draw back, always ineffectiveness. Concerning all acts of initiative (and creation), there is one elementary truth the ignorance of which kills countless ideas and splendid plans."

"The moment one definitely commits oneself, then providence moves too. All sorts of things occur to help one that would never otherwise have occurred. A whole stream of events issues from the decision, raising in one's favor all manner of unforeseen incidents and meetings and material assistance, which no man could have dreamed would have come his way. Whatever you can do, or dream you can, begin it. Boldness has genius, power and magic in it."

Begin it now.

Johann Wolfgang Von Goethe

www.ingramcontent.com/pod-product-compliance
Lightning Source LLC
LaVergne TN
LVHW061224100826
845148LV00004B/849

* 9 7 8 1 4 4 9 5 2 0 5 6 4 *